The Armed Discussion in Your Church

Daniel B. Blevins

ISBN-10: 1539612449
ISBN-13: 978-1539612445

CONTENTS

NOTICE

The information provided in this book is intended to be helpful in deciding how to proceed in developing your safety/security team. It does not constitute legal advice and is not a substitute for the counsel from a licensed attorney in your area.

1 THE COMMON QUESTION

"Should we have armed security in our church or not?" is a question that is becoming more of a topic of discussion in today's culture. Churches are a leading soft target in America for a terrorist attack, or for violent incidents perpetrated by people with mental health issues. As I talk with a variety of churches in America, there are several common themes when it comes to the safety and security of the congregation as a whole, and with respect to developing, training, and arming a security ministry in a church.

I will provide a lot of information as I build the case for an armed response in your church. This information helps explain why the answer is not simply either yes or no. There are many issues to consider and things to have in place before firearms are introduced into the mix.

Many churches believe things like: it won't happen to us; weapons don't belong in the church; we have people in the congregation that carry concealed that would respond (this will be addressed later); we don't want to create fear in the congregation by having a security ministry; and a number of others that may not have been considered carefully.

So, I think one of the best places for us to start is in the Bible. For many of us the Bible is considered to be the authority on all matters related to what we do in our churches. Although I recognize that there are other religious beliefs that do not use the Bible but are just as easily targets as the Christian churches in America.

You may be surprised to find out that the Bible actually has much to say about church security. Let's look at a few examples:

1 Chronicles 9:21-24 is a great verse that not only demonstrates the use of security for the house of worship but is also tactically wise: Zechariah *the son of Meshelemiah was gatekeeper at the entrance of the tent of meeting. All these, who were chosen as gatekeepers at the thresholds, were 212. They were enrolled by genealogies in their villages. David and Samuel the seer established them in their office of trust. So they and their sons were in charge of the gates of the house of the* Lord, *that is, the house of the tent, as guards. The gatekeepers were on the four sides, east, west, north, and south.*

Nehemiah 4:10-23 is a favorite one because it shows that there were men standing on the wall watching over the people doing the work of the Lord: In *Judah it was said, "The strength of those who bear the burdens is failing. There is too much rubble. By ourselves we will not be able to rebuild the wall." And our enemies said, "They will not know or see till we come among them and kill them and stop the work."[2] At that time the Jews who lived near them came from all directions and said to us ten times, "You must return to us." So in the lowest parts of the space behind the wall, in open places, I stationed the people by their clans, with their swords, their spears, and their bows. And I looked and arose and said to the nobles and to the officials and to the rest of the people, "Do not be afraid of them. Remember the Lord, who is* *great and awesome, and fight for your brothers, your sons, your daughters, your wives, and your homes." When our enemies heard that it was known to us and that God had frustrated their plan, we all returned to the wall, each to his work. From that day on, half of my servants worked on construction, and half held the spears, shields, bows, and coats of mail. And the leaders stood behind the whole house of Judah, who were building on the wall. Those who carried burdens were loaded in such a way that each labored on the work with one hand and held his weapon with the other. And each of the builders had his sword strapped at his side while he built. The man who sounded the trumpet was beside me. And I said to the nobles and to the officials and to the rest of the people, "The work is great and widely spread, and we are separated on the wall, far from one another. In the place where you hear the sound of the trumpet, rally to us there. Our God will fight for us." So we labored at the work, and half of them held the spears from the break of dawn until the stars came out. I also said to the people at that time, "Let every man and his servant pass the night within Jerusalem, that they may be a guard for us by night and may labor by day." So neither I nor my brothers nor my servants nor the men of the guard who followed me, none of us took off our clothes; each kept his weapon at his right hand.*

Luke 11:21 is one example of Jesus illustrating the importance of being armed: *When a strong man, fully armed, guards his own palace, his goods are safe;*

Luke 22:36 is another example from Jesus that has been often overlooked: *He said to them, "But now let the one who has a moneybag take it, and likewise a knapsack. And let the one who has no sword sell his cloak and buy one.*

These verses illustrate the importance of guarding the house of worship (the church). Although it seems like church security (and particularly armed security) is a new concept, the Bible shows us that God recognized the need to protect His house and His people.

2 MISTAKES MADE

Among the mistakes well-meaning churches make when introducing firearms into a security ministry there are some patterns that reoccur. This chapter aims to reveal those patterns so that others can learn from and avoid the same mistakes.

The "Who Has a Concealed Carry Permit?" Mistake

One church that we have worked with that started their security team by making an announcement to the congregation "If anyone here has a concealed gun permit, we need you to join the security team." Out of approximately 20 people that served on this team, there were only 8 that showed up for training.

We believe there are two key mistakes built into this approach. First, we think it is important that all volunteers get vetted for good temperament and sound judgment before they earn team membership through training. Second, we believe the whole security team should undergo training together, both to ensure a common knowledge and skill base and to help the group form into a team, familiar with one another.

We have seen this same mistake among other churches around the country. Most everyone in these situations has just enough training to get their certificate for their concealed permit. We will repeatedly call these people "Certificate Holders". Recruiting team members based solely or mainly on their status as Certificate Holders will feed into the pride of the person that has the permit, but it probably will not bring the person into your team that has the necessary judgment to handle the variety of situations that will occur.

Several years ago, there was a church that announced that they were going to have a meeting regarding the start of a security team. When the evening came for the meeting the location was fairly full with a variety of people that wanted to join this team. A large percentage of these people were only interested in being able to carry a gun in service to the church. Once they found out that they would not be able to carry a gun they were no longer interested in serving.

Much of this speaks to the heart and mindset of the person that will serve in your church. Are they the type of person that will be willing to pick up the towel to wash people's feet or are they the type that are there for themselves and the recognition that serving in this capacity might bring to them?

The "We Have People" Mistake

Another, similar situation that I encounter with churches is they firmly believe that there are people in the congregation who are armed and will step up if something were to happen. The dangerous assumption behind this belief is that people who have firearms, even those with no security training, will somehow know what to do and do the right thing in a dangerous circumstance. (The singular exception to this belief would be off duty law enforcement personnel.) We see multiple problems with this line of thinking.

- Most of these "Certificate Holders" have not been trained on how to handle shooting situations that involve crowded areas.
- Most people do not know what is going to happen to their body when they are in a dangerous situation or how to handle these changes their body is going to go through, including tunnel vision, loss of dexterity, etc.
- These people are taking a risk of getting shot themselves by an off duty officer or a responding officer. Their presence and behavior can also be an issue if the church or ministry has a trained safety and security team in place.

The "It Won't Happen to Us" Mistake

Really? How do you know? Evil can and does happen anytime and anywhere. Saying that it is not going to happen to you or your ministry is magic thinking at best, and negligent leadership.

Mark 1:21-23 (MSG) ".... Jesus lost no time getting to the meeting place. He spent the day there teaching... Suddenly, while still _in the meeting place_, he was interrupted by a man who was deeply disturbed and yelling out..." If the services were disturbed while Jesus was preaching, what makes people think that Satan won't interrupt yours? Just like in our own lives, the more impactful our churches are for the Kingdom of God, the more attacks Satan will have against us.

This _mental block_ has been created by a _faulty belief that says "Faith protects us from harm"_. When in fact the Bible has just the opposite to say about this.

Matthew 5:45 (ESV) "...For he makes his sun rise on the evil and on the good, and sends rain on the just and on the unjust."

Jesus even warned us of violence happening in our houses of

worship when He said:

Matthew 10:17 (ESV) "Beware of men, for they will deliver you over to courts and flog you *in* their *synagogues*…" Jesus is exposing the fact that the day is coming when criminals don't care where they cause harm.

In **Proverbs 22:3 (NLT)** "A prudent person foresees danger and takes precautions. The simpleton goes blindly on and suffers the consequences". A prudent person would recognize that evil and danger is an any time – any place opportunity.

There are people who believe that their building is protected because God dwells there. Does he really? There are many verses that show that this is not the case, and here is one good example:

Acts 7:48-51 (MSG) "Yet that doesn't mean that the Most High God lives in a building made by carpenters and masons." The prophet Isaiah put it well when he wrote, "Heaven is my throne room; I rest my feet on earth. So what kind of house will you build me?" says God. "Where I can get away and relax? It's already built, and I built it." "And you continue, so bullheaded! Calluses on your hearts, flaps on your ears! Deliberately ignoring the Holy Spirit, you're just like your ancestors."

The "Satan Won't Bring Evil to the House of God" Mistake

This is a common thought among church leaders. In October of 2016 there was a shooting at a church in Peoria, Illinois after which the church leader reportedly said, "We are infuriated that the devil had the audacity to come to this house of God and perform these acts." Really? God does not dwell in a building that man has made.

Acts 17:24-25 *The God who made world and everything in it, being Lord of heaven and earth, does not live in temples made by man, nor is he served by human hands, as though he needs anything, since he himself gives to all mankind life and breath and everything.* Again we see what God thinks of this kind of thinking in.

Acts 7:49-51 *Heaven is my throne, and the earth is my footstool. What kind of house will you build for me, says the Lord, or what is the place of my rest? Did not my hands make all these things? You stiff-necked people, uncircumcised in heart and ears, you always resist the Holy Spirit. As your fathers did, so do you.*

God is very clear on what he thinks of this way of thinking. This can be a very dangerous way of thinking for a congregation by a church leader. The body of Christ is the believers and followers that are attending their congregations.

Some Statistics

Let's look at some statistics about evil against churches and ministries. All of these data are current through June 2016 and can be accessed and verified through Carl Chinn, whose data goes back to 1999. (www.carlchinn.com).

We are assured in the Bible that this is not going to get better but is going to continue to get worse over time. One reason that we do not see these data trending higher is because medical treatment continues to get better preventing the death toll from running closer to the incident numbers.

This first chart depicts the incidents verses deaths since 1999. Notice that the incidents and death trends continue to rise over time. The data for individual years are not so important as the trend of steadily increasing violent incidents and deaths.

INCIDENT/DEATH TRENDS IN CHURCHES
UPDATED 12/05/2017

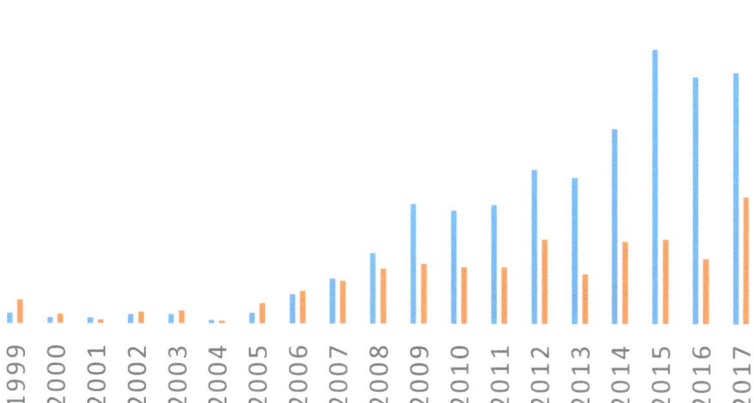

People don't realize that there is more violence in our churches then there is in our schools. The schools continue to improve as they harden themselves against these and other types of violent acts. So, what is it going to take for the churches of our country to realize that this is a serious issue and that it can't be ignored any longer? If the churches don't prepare and prepare properly the violence will continue to rise.

This next chart depicts the total numbers of incidents and deaths in houses of worship 1999 - 2016. To put these numbers into perspective, and compare them to school shootings that we get bombarded with by the press when they happen, since 1980 – 2012 there have been 137 incidents that resulted in 297 deaths in schools and colleges. It is hard to get accurate data on schools without bias.

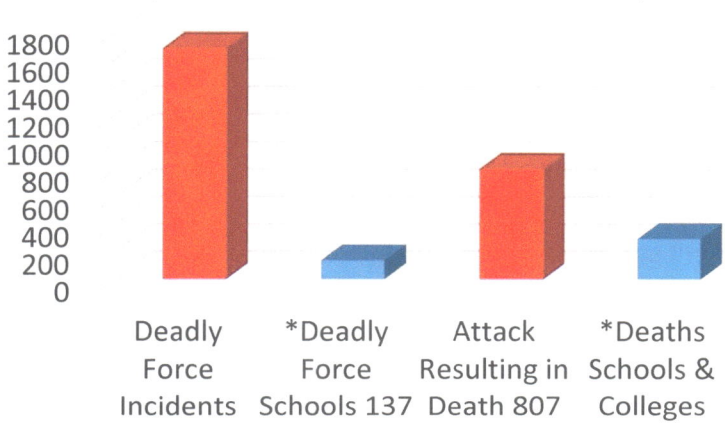

Deadly Force Incidents in Churches 1999-11/2017

*School Data through 2012. Insufficient data since.

This next chart shows violence by denomination. There are several factors that could contribute to one denomination having more incidents and others having less. For example, how outspoken a particular denomination is regarding controversial social issues may make a difference.

Another perspective to consider is that Satan is going to attack and be disruptive where God is moving and working in his people.

1 Peter 5:8 *Be sober minded; be watchful. Your adversary the devil prowls around like a roaring lion, seeking someone to devour.* The church is just a building and it is not where God dwells. He dwells in lives of followers. Satan has no reason to spend much time creating violence and disruptions if there are people who profess to believe (even Satan and his fallen angels do that!) but are not following Christ in an active and growing relationship that we are called to. That is a threat to Satan that he will attack. Just another perspective to consider.

Violence by Denomination

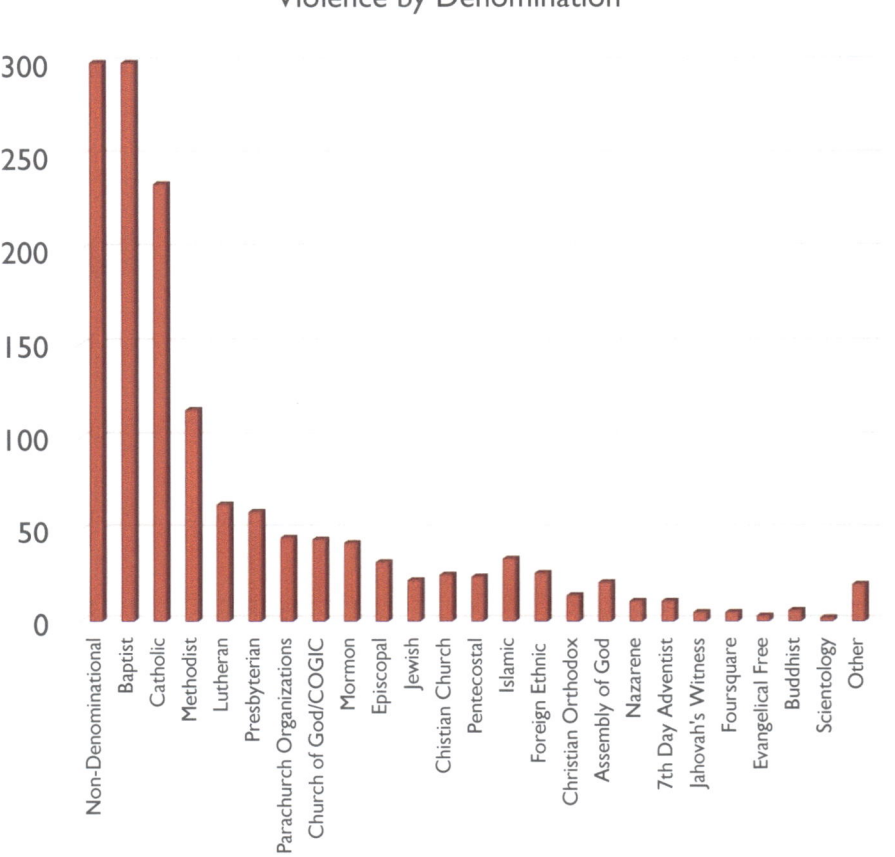

We maintain many more charts and statistics that go into greater detail, but the final one that I want to address speaks to the core subject of this booklet; weapons used in incidents. It does not matter what instrument of violence is used; anything can be deadly. So as you have looked at the previous statistics and the next chart a good question you might have to ask about yourself or your congregation is "Am I doing what is necessary to be ready?"

Incident Weapons

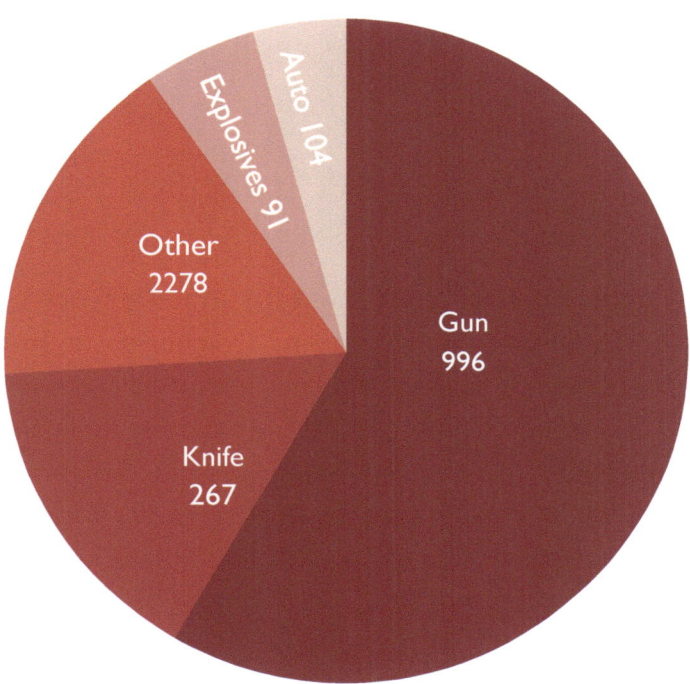

3 TEAM DEVELOPMENT

Before I get into greater detail about the armed response, let's start with the foundation of the team. I will begin with that church that does not yet have a team established and then take a closer look at a church that may already have a team in place. Maybe you have a few people in the congregation that carry a concealed firearm and perhaps the thinking is that they would respond if something were to happen. (I will discuss these people later).

No Team Yet: The Invite

Before recruiting any team members, it is essential to gain both the support financial and the ministerial commitment of the church leadership, not only the pastor(s) but also the church board. So, I begin with the assumption that this support and commitment is in place.

Recruit with the Jesus approach. When I look how Jesus selected the men that were to be with Him, He did not make any announcements as to what He was doing. He invited each person to join Him on this great adventure. He handpicked the men that He wanted on His team.

 John 15:16 "You did not choose me, but I chose you and appointed you that you should go and bear fruit and that your fruit should abide...."

Why shouldn't we follow this same example when it comes to who is allowed to represent the church, and protect its flock, in this capacity?

I recommend inviting men and women in your church that you feel have the right temperament and judgment necessary to serve in this capacity. When you invite them, are clear the invitation is to attend an informational meeting, and there will be additional steps in forming a security ministry team.

These people are about to be commissioned by the church as ambassadors and representatives of the church. The persons that you want to invite should meet the same criteria that is listed for elders in **Titus 1:5-9:** *[5] This is why I left you in Crete, so that you might put what remained into order, and appoint elders in every town as I directed you— [6] if anyone is above reproach, the husband of one wife, and his children are believers and not open to the charge of debauchery or insubordination. [7] For an overseer, as God's steward, must be above reproach. He must not be arrogant or quick-tempered or a drunkard or violent or greedy for gain, [8] but hospitable, a lover of good, self-controlled, upright, holy, and disciplined. [9] He must hold firm to the trustworthy word as taught, so that he may be able to give instruction in sound[l] doctrine and also to rebuke those who contradict it.*

Why are these standards so important for this ministry? These are the people that are going to put themselves on the frontline for of all ministries. If Satan wants to attack and cause weakness in the defenses of the church, these are the people that will bear the brunt of that attack.

In the informational meeting, take steps to ensure that anyone chosen to move forward to the next steps understands the significance of the responsibility they may undertake. They must understand that their focus needs to be on the vertical relationship with God so that the horizontal falls into place, not only in this area of service but also in all areas of their life where Satan will try to bring them down.

No Team Yet: Initial Training

It is important to keep in mind that these people that are going to be serving in this capacity are volunteers. You want to be respectful of the time that they are giving to serve. So, come to the training with a well-prepared agenda, and adhere to the time allotments you plan.

There may be people on the team that already have their concealed carry permit. I often refer to these people as certificate holders, because many of them have just enough training to get the certificate in order to get the permit. This initial training time is not the time for these certificate holders to bring their firearms. Explain that perhaps you will ask them to bring their weapons for a particular training reason at a later date. (When to introduce firearms into the training process is a topic covered later.)

Ideally, prior to this initial training time, some initial policies and procedures have been developed. This training is the time to give each member the policies and procedures that have been established prior to the training. Let each of them know that they may change from time to time as situations and climate changes. Tell them that you value their input in the development of these and future policies and procedures.

This initial training is a meet and greet time for each of the team members. It is always good to have some sort of refreshment on hand during all trainings as appropriate to the time of day for the training, because many participants may come from busy times at work or at home, and may not have had time to eat beforehand.

This would also be the time to let them know what the format of future training would look like. The best way to put your training together is to develop a training plan that can be duplicable for future use. To engage those that have been serving for a long time, new ideas and tools should be used to stretch the team in their learning and abilities. You might also ask these experienced hands to describe best practices and lessons learned from their prior service. The subjects that are necessary for training will be discussed in chapter two.

Already Have a Team: Cleaning House
Maybe you have been the leader of this team for some time and now realize that you may not have approached this ministry well, or that you have people on the team that really should not be on the team. These members could be people who are only on the team because they have been allowed to carry a firearm and it makes them feel important to be able to do so. Maybe you have people that have not demonstrated good judgment in tense situations, or are constantly unable to accept the authority of those appointed over them in this ministry. You have been conducting "training" and but the same people never show up because they believe that it is not necessary. Maybe you have people on the team whose walk with God is far from what it should be and therefore they do not meet the requirements in Titus 1.

 As the leader you might have to make the hard decisions.   If you see a pathway forward through changes in their behavior, first ask them to step up to what is expected. Be clear about what you expect them to do, how you expect that their behavior will change.

If they decline to make changes, or if you do not see a way forward, the conversation might go something like "We thank you for your service but we are going to ask you to step down at this time. I can take your key and credentials at this time." You should document the dismissal in a letter, diplomatically written, and filed for formal recordkeeping.

Actions like this can be tough, might be especially stressful if you have people in leadership that are not fully backing this ministry, or do that do not fully understand the importance of high standards for those who serve on the security team. Conversations with leadership prior to taking action to remove people from the team would be advisable if you anticipate the potential for backlash from your actions.

Already Have a Team: Next Steps
If your situation does not meet *all* of the following criteria, then I urge you to suspend the carrying of firearms on church property:

1. You have been conducting advanced firearms training monthly, requiring a qualification shoot every 6 months.
2. You have training records that document all training conducted, including written attendance records, e.g. sign-in sheets, that show who has attended.
3. You have a Letter of Appointment from church leadership for each member who has met the necessary standards.
4. You have a specific insurance rider for their protection, and the protection of the church.

If you have lost some team members in this process or feel that you need to add more team members, now is the time to do a personal invitation to those in the church that you feel that meet the necessary standards address above. If you don't make a "blanket" announcement to your congregation, you will not have as many people to discharge for having a lack of a servant's attitude but rather are there to fulfill a potential selfish and prideful motivation. Somebody might ask to join the team and that would be ok after an interview and probationary period.

As mentioned in the No Team Yet sections, establishing a training routine that is duplicable is important. Review the above sections regarding training. Since these are volunteers, the training will seem repetitive over time. That is ok because like many things in life, you have to keep repeating the actions in order for them to become second nature.

Remind people that one of the purposes of the training is to ensure they feel confident about how to react in situations that may demand a response with deadly force in a matter of seconds.

4 THE NECESSARY TOOLS

When we are working with churches and ministries we establish early on that the armed response is the *last* resort and the odds of ever needing it are pretty long.

Even though the probability is small, the fact remains that they may come a time when an armed response is justified, even imperative.

Training is the preparation that will make or break a response to a crisis situation. A crisis situation could be a medical emergency, someone disrupting a service, a person wandering the parking lot, a couple who brought their domestic problems to the church, etc. The potential scenarios that could occur are virtually unlimited. Let's discuss the different training topics that need to be part of your training plan.

Verbal Skills
Law enforcement experts call this Verbal Judo. Designed to de-escalate situations, these techniques should be taught to proficiency and reinforced on a constant basis. Every training session should have verbal de-escalation as part of their training agenda. Perhaps you will find it helpful to incorporate recent, actual situations into the training, both to make it realistic and to

keep it fresh. Debriefing an incident with the security team can afford excellent learning opportunities.

Most everything that you encounter on your church or ministry property will require good verbal skills to handle the situation correctly. Everyone on the team needs this training, with frequent refreshers, so that when a situation arises, each person knows what the other is going to do in that particular situation so they can support their teammates correctly.

Take Verbal Judo training very seriously, as it is the often the foundation of what we do not only in ministry but also in life. If we don't communicate well, situations can go downhill very quickly.

When situations get tense, even critical, what we say and how we say it makes all the difference. These skills start with helping to gain understanding of the situation or the issues involved. Another key skill set focuses on gaining compliance without escalation to higher levels of intervention. Often we help people get the necessary help that they ultimately desire from the church, perhaps even their primary reason for being there. These skills involve both listening and gathering information from observations of non-verbal behavior.

It is impossible to over-emphasize the importance of learning, refining, regularly practicing and constantly improving these skills.

Defensive Tactics

Much like the verbal skills, Defensive Tactics are another set of skills that one does not learn in one class session. These skills too should be practiced each time you get together for training.

A verbal confrontation or conflict can escalate quickly and you will need the necessary skills to defend yourself while subduing the attacker.

Defensive Tactics skills, if taught properly, can also aide you in removing someone that is disruptive from your worship center or meeting rooms who is unwilling to leave on their own when asked. If taught and practiced properly, Defensive Tactics can be applied in such a way that they appear to be defensive instead of offensive. That difference is often important when others review the situation later, especially if there is a video record.

If your team does not have the Defensive Tactics skills necessary to combine with the verbal skills, to apply when the situation calls for a physical response, and they are carrying a firearm, they are going to see their firearm as the only option that they have. The more options that you can train for the better.

Medical Training

Medical crises are statistically more likely to happen in your church than violence. It is important that each person on the team is First Aid, CPR, and AED certified. Your facility should have at least one trauma bag that can be reached easily. Your facility should have at least one AED easily accessible in an emergency. Ensuring the right kits and equipment are in the right place at the right time requires an assessment of your individual church or ministry. I can work closely with you to provide that assessment.

There are several churches that I have talked with that say they have a medical team. This can be a good thing if your state or county allows such interventions based on a Good Samaritan Law, a law that protects them if they try to help by not jeopardizing the careers of those that are serving on that team.

Regardless of whether there is a medical team, each person serving on the safety and security team should still have the necessary training to be able to respond until professionals can arrive. In the minutes it takes for professionals to respond, a well-trained person can make a huge difference, even a lifesaving difference.

A church should also consider expanding this medical training to other areas of ministry. A medical emergency can happen at any time and very quickly. A children's worker, usher, greeter, church staff, etc. that are sufficiently trained could respond to an emergency for someone in their care or nearby until the professionals arrived.

Firearm Training

For many of you, this is the section you anticipated the most. Please, notice that we address firearms training last because it should always be the last resort. That was very intentional.

We cannot overemphasize that an armed response is always the last option.

I understand that the discussion of firearms in a church or ministry is something that people in your church or ministry may not be willing to even discuss right away.

We would just ask that you consider preparing an armed response as an option. In the unlikely event that you need an organized armed response, from people who are well trained and temperamentally suited, it will obviously be too late to provide one.

When an individual or individuals enter a building with firearms to cause harm to those in the building, in most cases the incident is over in two minutes or less. Having the right people properly trained in the correct areas can prevent this from happening almost every time. They may not be able to keep everyone from getting hurt but they can prevent more people from getting hurt.

As mentioned earlier, many of the people that want to volunteer to carry a firearm in the church have little more qualifications than the minimal training necessary to get a concealed carry permit. They may go to a range occasionally and shoot at a round paper target. These limited activities do not develop the necessary skills to intervene judiciously and effectively with a firearm.

I would recommend that if you are going to have an armed element to your safety and security team, that the training that you do for these individuals is conducted on a different day of the month. You may have members on your team that want to serve but do not want to train or carry a firearm. There are important roles for these volunteers, and there are ample topics previously listed to fill the normal monthly training.

I would recommend that you conduct firearms training on an evening when your buildings are not in use or when there is little enough use that others will not interfere with the necessary moving tactics and empty firearm practice in the building.

This firearms skills training should also occur monthly. It is good to start with the basics of firearms safety and build from there to include topics such as proper equipment, tactical reloads, combat reloads, communication, room clearing, and move and shoot tactics, among others. Much of the impact of this training is to create the muscle memory necessary so that when the adrenaline is pumping and the tunnel vision is upon them, they know what to expect and how to persevere through it all.

Your church may need to repeat this training for a while to get everyone up to speed. You should require a documented range qualification test. Often times this test might look like a variation of an off duty officer qualification. Dry fire training is great and should form the foundation of firearms qualification, but there needs to be some live fire training if there is someplace in your community that will allow that to happen.

When there has been in a lapse in our range time due to other obligations it will be evident that our skills have gotten a bit rusty. Require firearms training at least a couple of times a month. Even that frequently, the impact of the training increases substantially if a mentor works with each qualifier to maintain safety and sound technique.

Like many things that we do in life, if we don't practice, we will lose that skill. Military and law enforcement teams who train to handle active shooter situations train, and re-train and then train some more. They may literally spend more than 95% of their active time training rather than responding to a real crisis.

Scenario Based Training

Keeping in mind that you are working with volunteers that are not usually active or prior law enforcement. These volunteers therefore, lack opportunities to use the skills that they are learning. They need scenario based training to ingrain the skills so that they can apply them in moments of crisis and tension.

Begin with easy scenarios that focus on one skill first. Use something to record a video of how the members perform in the scenario.

Start with verbal skills. Maybe you bring in different "actors" to roll play. Perhaps you have someone play a parent entering into the children's area determined to get their child out of their classroom. He or she has not presented the necessary documents to have that child released to them. But, the actor/parent insists that it is their weekend and that it is time for that child to come with them. This example allows for the team members to be able to use the verbal skills that they have been learning to de-escalate the situation. The "actors" should become cooperative once good verbal skills are used.

This training provides a situation in which it is ok to fail. Using the recordings for debriefing and feedback will give everyone a chance to learn from each other to improve their verbal skills. Once everyone is doing well with the first skill, you can move on and insert the next skill, a more complex skill to learn and apply.

Next, escalate the situation. Returning to the parent-child scenario above, to progress to the next level after the verbal skills have been applied well, ask the parent-actor to not cooperate with the safety and security team members. Now you insert the defensive tactics that they have learned for these types of situations. After recording, reviewing, and learning from the mistakes that will happen, then you can escalate the training to incorporate the parent with a weapon.

It is good to get the other ministries involved in the training as well: the greeters, ushers, parking attendants, worship participants, children's staff and volunteers among others, to name just a few. Similar training should be designed and accomplished with the staff, focusing on what they need to do when called upon to respond and handle situations that may arise while they are there during the week.

5 WHAT NOW?

Hopefully by now you might realize that there are several stages that need to happen before the armed component is introduced into the recipe of a safety and security team. There are additional subjects to consider for the team in general and for the armed component that we have not discussed yet. We have talked about the importance of specific training, but if you decide to allow the armed component as part of your safety and security team here are a few additional items to consider.

Insurance Rider

Most of the major insurance companies for churches have an insurance policy rider option. Many churches that I talk with have not considered this vital piece of the safety and security structure.

Knowing your insurance agent and having conversations with that agent as your team develops is important for the protection of the volunteers as well as the church. For instance, a good rider on the church's insurance will provide the church and your volunteers primary coverage, and not be secondary to the volunteers own homeowner's liability coverage.

Some critical questions to ask your insurance agent about the possibility that a safety team member could injure someone include:

- Who exactly is covered?
- What does the policy/rider language say about intentional acts exclusion?
- What does it say about the use of force?
- Is there anything that would cause a denial of coverage?
- Does the policy include – or specifically exclude – coverage for armed security operations?
- What if an innocent bystander were shot, what does the policy cover?

These are only a few examples of questions that should be asked. Perhaps it would be helpful to seek the voluntary assistance of an attorney who is familiar with these liability issues and the insurance to protect the church against them.

In the course of reviewing your coverage and asking these questions, seek answers on what a general liability policy would cover, and whether the church would have to get additional coverage that would cover:

- Primary Coverage for Team Members
- Modification of Intentional Acts Exclusion
- Emotional Distress Coverage
- Higher Medical Expense Limits
- Wage Loss Reimbursement
- Post-Incident Counseling Coverage

Training Specifics

There are some things that you need to consider having in place in order to have good organization. Having these items in place will also help you to prove that you have organized training and clear standards in place.

- Training Records – Establishing training records for each person on the team will help you know who is trained and what they are trained to do. It is ok to use a spreadsheet or something similar to track some of the specifics, but keep in mind that should an incident happen police/ lawyers would want to see everything printed out for each person. I am not a big fan of paper, but when it comes to training records I am a stickler for having a file folder for each person that is on the team. Experience teaches that when you need the records, it's too late to create records that will have any credibility.

- o Information to have in the records would include:
    - CPR/AED/First Aid Training
    - Letter of Appointment – This is a document that is provided for each person on the team that authorizes to act on behalf of the church in the capacity of safety and security. This document needs to be specific to what capacity they are authorized to serve (i.e. carry a firearm).
    - Training certificates they may go get on their own (i.e. NRA Instructor, Range Safety Officer, Etc.)
    - If they have been given keys or similar to access the church, having a document that identifies what they have and what authority they have to use it.
    - Anything else that shows their training and service.
    - For each of the above, dates of initial training and re-training (or certification), where and by whom.
- Training Plan – Design a training plan for all aspects of training. This training plan should be something that is duplicable each year. Here are some things that it should

include. This is just a short list of ideas and CorrValues can help you develop these training components.
- o   Verbal De-Escalation Training
- o   Defensive Tactics
- o   Basic Firearms
- o   Advanced Firearm Training
- o   Simulated responses to a variety of Scenarios
- o   CPR/AED/First Aid
- o   Recognizing mental illnesses

The Armed Component Training

This aspect of training is something that requires some special consideration. There are key skills that everyone who carries a firearm should have. Again we emphasize our belief that everyone that decides to carry concealed should have more skill sets then just what they learned in the class to get their certificate before they join a security ministry team as an armed protector.

Much of this training can be accomplished in a dry fire situation in order to help develop the necessary muscle memory so that when the adrenaline and tunnel vision creep up on them during a critical incident they have the necessary skills drilled into them to be able to battle through. Each person needs to take the responsibility for their own skills and be able to demonstrate them when called upon to do so.

This training time should also be used to evaluate the gear that each person is using with their firearm(s), including holsters and extra magazines. If the equipment is not working for them smoothly, then during training is the time to discover that issue and get reliable equipment. It is vital that you have the correct equipment that performs reliably for you *every* time.

Therefore, the number one lesson each person carrying a firearm must learn is to keep their weapon clean, well lubricated and in top working order. A jammed firearm is no more useful than a paperweight.

I would recommend dedicating additional training time to those that are authorized to carry a firearm in the ministry of safety and security. It is advisable to establish a requirement for a live fire qualification that must be maintained at least twice a year to stay qualified. Using your town's off duty officer qualification as a starting place would be good.

Once the proper caliber, gear, and basics listed above are met then it is time to elevate the challenge to some more tactical and scenario based training. However, if the person serving does not have the proper gear, caliber, and established muscle memory of the basic skills, any kind of tactical scenario-based training will be ineffective.

The information provided here is only a small portion of the items that have to be considered when moving forward with a safety and security team and especially if you are going to add an armed component to that team. If you already have that armed component, you might want to put it on pause and make sure that you have everything in place in order to protect the volunteer, church, and church staff.

6 PULLING IT TOGETHER

We started off with a question that only you can answer for your church. "Should we have armed security in our church or not?" I hope that as you have read this booklet you have a better understanding that this is not the simple yes or no question that many believe it to be.

I would also encourage you, your church leadership, etc. to prayerfully consider everything that I have discussed here. None of us should take this decision quickly or lightly. Failing to bring God into the process and acting on your own no more advisable here, than it is in so many other aspects of your life.

Yes Answer

If the answer for you is YES, that you should have an armed component, I would encourage you to do everything necessary to protect those that are serving in that capacity and to protect the church. Carrying a firearm in any capacity comes with great responsibility in our society and even more so in a church safety and security ministry. You want to choose people for your team that understand this obligation and live it daily.

Inviting people that you know who have good judgment and who are able to remain calm in high stress situations is going to be one key to the success for any security effort, especially an armed component. As mentioned previously, training is a component that is vital for the many reasons given above. Proper documentation of training and having a good training plan and standards will help keep everyone focused and energized to learn more.

Make sure that you are avoiding the mistakes we listed above, and ask yourself how confident you feel that you and your church are ready to move forward and not make other mistakes on your own. Know that you can reach out to CV Ministries and we will help you in your situation.

Every church is unique and requires individual consultation to make sure you are getting it right. In the next section there are a variety of items that are critical no matter which choice you make.

No Answer

If the answer for you is NO, that you do not believe that it is right for your church to have an armed component, I would encourage you to make sure that you are providing the necessary training the people who work or volunteer at your church. Look at the training in such a way that you are working from the outside to the inside. Some examples would be:

- Parking lot attendants
- Greeters
- Ushers
- Children's Workers
- Sound/Video Technicians
- Worship Team/Choir
- Pastor
- Weekly staff in the offices
- Etc.

You can plug a variety of different ministries into this list to fit your specific needs.

I would also encourage you to develop the necessary policy and procedures that articulate what to do in a variety of emergency situations to include:

- Natural Disaster
- Disruption to the service
- Office access during the week
- Violent attack
- Domestic spillover
- Medical emergency
- Fire
- Etc.

The list could be nearly endless but does not have to be. You cannot prepare for every possible situation. But, by being prepared and conducting training for many situations, when one arises that you may not have trained for, your ability respond a correct and effective way is more likely than having never prepared.

Where do I stand in these choices? I stand on the side of the YES. I believe that no matter how slight the risk is; I believe that we are called to be prepared with all of the considerations that I have mentioned. Knowing that I have the skills and ability to prevent or stop evil and elect to do nothing would make it tough for me to live with myself. I won't tell anyone what it right for them and will continue to train churches and ministries in ways that work best for them.

Finally, I would advise having the necessary communications procedures in place. In the aftermath of an incident, you or a designated representative can articulate to the congregation, law enforcement, your attorney, the district attorney, and a court of law, etc. specifics regarding the policy choices you have made.

Failing to be prepared is not an option, so do everything you can to be prepared. Failing to be prepared when you knew you should be will not end will for you, church leadership, and the church.

ABOUT THE AUTHOR

Daniel earned a Bachelor's of Science in Management degree from the University of Phoenix, and retired from the U.S. Air Force in 2007 after 21 years. His experience in the Air Force included security details and training in security procedures, which equipped him to understand and implement safety and security processes and procedures in ministries and churches. Daniel trained Air Force units throughout the United States on a variety of issues, including policy and procedures, and organizational management, which allows him to provide effective training to ministries and churches.

Daniel was a founding member of the Woodmen Valley Chapel church security team. Woodmen is a multi-site, mega church that Brotherhood Mutual Insurance Company consulted and cited in their church security manual. Daniel was involved in developing the policy, procedures, and practices of the Woodmen Valley Chapel church security team. Since joining CorrValues, LLC as the Church Security Director, he has been instrumental in developing safety and security programs for other churches and ministries. In addition to his experience developing the church security team at Woodmen, Daniel has managed the facilities at the 5 building campus that typically hosts 4,000 to 5,000 people every weekend and multiple activities throughout the week. This experience enables him to assess and help ensure the safety of the buildings and campuses of churches and ministries. He has over 20 years of handgun experience, has trained in verbal de-escalation, defensive tactics, and lethal and non–lethal response. Daniel holds a NRA Pistol Instructor Certification along with NRA Range Safety Officer Certification. He has developed policies, procedures, and training to ensure a highly qualified safety and security program.